·TELL ME ABOUT

AIR, LIGHT & WATER

By Mary-Jane Wilkins
Illustrated by Chris Forsey

RANDOM HOUSE   NEW YORK

First American edition, 1991

Copyright © 1990 by Grisewood & Dempsey.
All rights reserved under International and Pan-
American Copyright Conventions. Published in the
United States by Random House, Inc., New York.
Originally published in Great Britain by Kingfisher
Books, a Grisewood & Dempsey Company, in 1990.

Library of Congress Cataloging-in-Publication Data
Wilkins, Mary-Jane.
    Air, light & water / by Mary-Jane Wilkins;
illustrated by Chris Forsey.
        p.   cm.—(Tell me about)
    Includes index.
    Summary: Questions and answers introduce
air, light, and water and the scientific principles
involving them.
    ISBN 0-679-80859-0
    1. Science—Juvenile literature. 2. Air—
Juvenile literature. 3. Light—Juvenile
literature. 4. Water—Juvenile literature.
[1. Air—Miscellanea. 2. Light—Miscellanea.
3. Water—Miscellanea. 4. Science—
Miscellanea. 5. Questions and answers.]
I. Forsey, Christopher, ill. II. Title. III. Title: Air,
Light, and water. IV. Series.
Q163.W512 1991
500—dc20   90-42620
                                    CIP
                                    AC
Manufactured in Spain   1 2 3 4 5 6 7 8 9 10

Contents

What is air made of?

Air is a mixture of gases which we cannot see, smell, or taste. Air is all around us, though – we can feel it as wind.

The three main gases in air are nitrogen, oxygen, and carbon dioxide. We need to breathe the oxygen gas to stay alive. In fact, all living things on Earth need oxygen. Without it they would die.

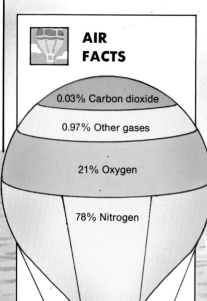

AIR FACTS

0.03% Carbon dioxide

0.97% Other gases

21% Oxygen

78% Nitrogen

• Air is largely made up of the gases nitrogen (78%) and oxygen (21%).

• Air also contains water in the form of a gas (called water vapor) plus tiny particles of salt, dust, and dirt.

Sailboats and sailboards move because their sails catch moving air, or wind.

4

Warm air is lighter than cold air, so it rises. Birds can float upward on rising currents of warm air. These currents are called thermals.

DO YOU KNOW

Air has weight, even though we don't notice it. The air pressing on 1 square inch of this book weighs 14.7 pounds. The air in an average single bedroom weighs about the same as a 7-year-old child – 48 pounds or so.

HIDDEN AIR

As well as being all around us, air fills up tiny spaces in all sorts of things. You can see this hidden air by putting different objects underwater and watching air bubbles escape.

1 Push a bottle underwater and let it fill up. Although the bottle looked empty, it was really full of air. As water rushed in, it pushed this air out. That's why you saw bubbles rising through the water.

2 Try some other objects. Push a clay flowerpot under the water. Then try a small amount of soil. Did the flowerpot and the soil have air in them?

3 See whether there is any air in water by leaving a glass of it in a warm place. After an hour or so, you'll see bubbles of air in the water and on the sides of the glass!

Is there air in space?

There is no air at all in space, only around Earth. The layer of air around Earth is called the atmosphere, and it is about 600 miles deep. Scientists divide the atmosphere into four bands — the troposphere (nearest to Earth), stratosphere, ionosphere, and exosphere.

? DO YOU KNOW

Compared with the size of Earth, the atmosphere is about as thick as the skin of a peach.

The atmosphere acts like a barrier, protecting us from the sun's heat as well as from its harmful rays.

Because there is no air in space, there is no oxygen for astronauts to breathe. They have to take tanks of oxygen with them when they work outside their spacecraft.

Why do climbers carry oxygen?

The amount of air in Earth's atmosphere varies – the higher you go, the less there is. People describe this as the air getting thinner. The less air there is, the less oxygen there is for breathing. That's why people who climb very high mountains, like Everest or Annapurna, usually take tanks of oxygen with them.

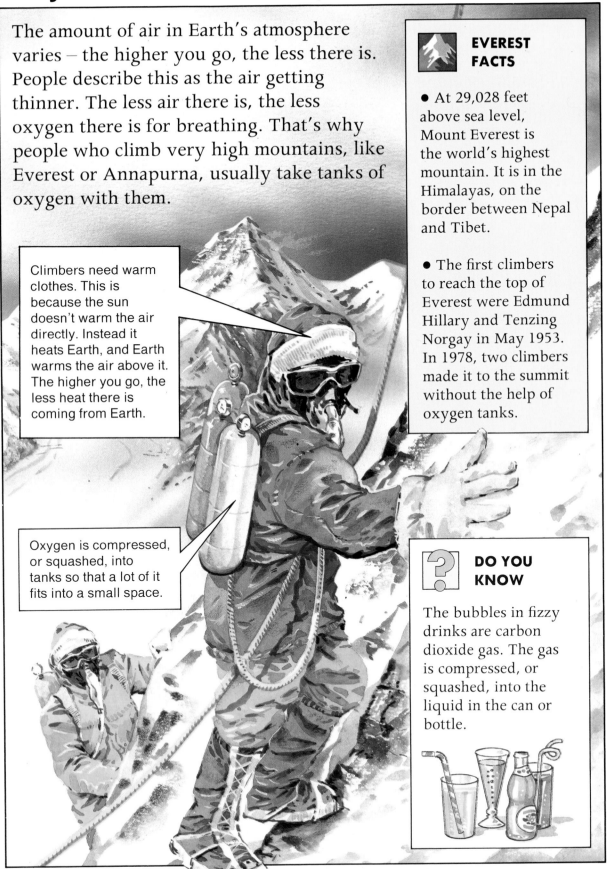

Climbers need warm clothes. This is because the sun doesn't warm the air directly. Instead it heats Earth, and Earth warms the air above it. The higher you go, the less heat there is coming from Earth.

Oxygen is compressed, or squashed, into tanks so that a lot of it fits into a small space.

EVEREST FACTS

● At 29,028 feet above sea level, Mount Everest is the world's highest mountain. It is in the Himalayas, on the border between Nepal and Tibet.

● The first climbers to reach the top of Everest were Edmund Hillary and Tenzing Norgay in May 1953. In 1978, two climbers made it to the summit without the help of oxygen tanks.

DO YOU KNOW

The bubbles in fizzy drinks are carbon dioxide gas. The gas is compressed, or squashed, into the liquid in the can or bottle.

Where does oxygen come from?

The oxygen our bodies take from the air when we breathe has to be replaced, or Earth would run out of it. This job is done by green plants, which produce oxygen in their leaves when they make food in sunlight.

If we cut down trees, they can't produce oxygen for us to breathe. Even so, many more are cut down than are planted – a forest the size of a football field is destroyed every second.

The green color of plant leaves and stems is produced by a sub-stance called chloro-phyll, which plants need to make their food. Sunlight acts with the chlorophyll in plant leaves to turn carbon dioxide gas from the air and water from the soil into food. At the same time the leaves give out oxygen. This whole process is called photosynthesis.

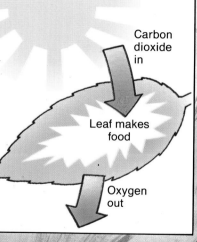

Carbon dioxide in

Leaf makes food

Oxygen out

? DO YOU KNOW

When we breathe in, we take air into our lungs. Oxygen gas from the air then passes into our bodies. We breathe out air containing more of two other gases – carbon dioxide and water vapor.

Can fires burn without air?

Fires use up oxygen from the air as they burn. They can't burn without it, which is why firefighters use water and other substances to put out fires – to try to stop the oxygen in air from reaching the flames. If a fire can't get enough oxygen, it dies.

 CANDLE RACE

1 Find out whether fire needs air. Ask an adult to help you light two candles, then cover one with a jar.

2 The covered candle will go out first, when it's used most of the oxygen in the jar.

When fires burn, they give out energy – light energy which you can see, and heat energy which you can feel keeping you warm.

 MAKE A FIRE EXTINGUISHER

Fire extinguishers work by stopping the oxygen in air from reaching the flames of a fire. Many use carbon dioxide gas, which is heavier than air and doesn't burn.

Here's a way to see how carbon dioxide fire extinguishers work.

Ask an adult to help you while you are doing this experiment.

1 Fix a candle to a saucer and light it.

2 Put 1 teaspoon of bicarbonate of soda into a glass and pour in about ½ ounce of vinegar. When these substances are mixed, carbon dioxide gas forms.

3 Hold a cardboard tube just above the candle flame. Carefully tip the glass and imagine you are pouring the heavy carbon dioxide gas down the tube. The flame will soon go out, as the carbon dioxide gas pushes the oxygen away from it.

Invisible carbon dioxide gas

Cardboard tube

What is wind power?

Wind is moving air, and people discovered ways of using its power hundreds of years ago. Early windmills ground corn into flour or pumped water from wells – as the wind turned the windmill's sails, the sails moved machinery inside the mill tower. Nowadays, wind turbines like the ones below are used to make electricity.

DO YOU KNOW

The USA has the most wind turbines in the world. About 15,000 have been built since the early 1980s.

WINDMILL FACTS

● Windmills were being used to grind grain in Asia 2,400 years ago. They were introduced to Europe in the 1100s.

● In the Netherlands, windmills have been used to pump water from low-lying land since the 1400s.

● The largest Dutch windmill has sails which measure nearly 100 feet across.

The world's largest wind turbine has blades 400 feet long. It's being built in Oahu, Hawaii.

Some wind turbines have blades that are shaped like the propeller on an airplane. To work well, the blades must be high off the ground and facing into the wind.

How does air help with flight?

Although we can't really feel it, air has pressure, or pushing power. A hang glider stays airborne because of the way air pressure works on the curved shape of its wing. The curve makes the air flowing over the wing move faster than the air under it. Because slow-moving air has more pressure than fast-moving air, the air beneath the wing has more push than the air above it. This lifts the hang glider and helps it to fly.

Birds glide with the aid of air pressure, in much the same way as hang gliders do.

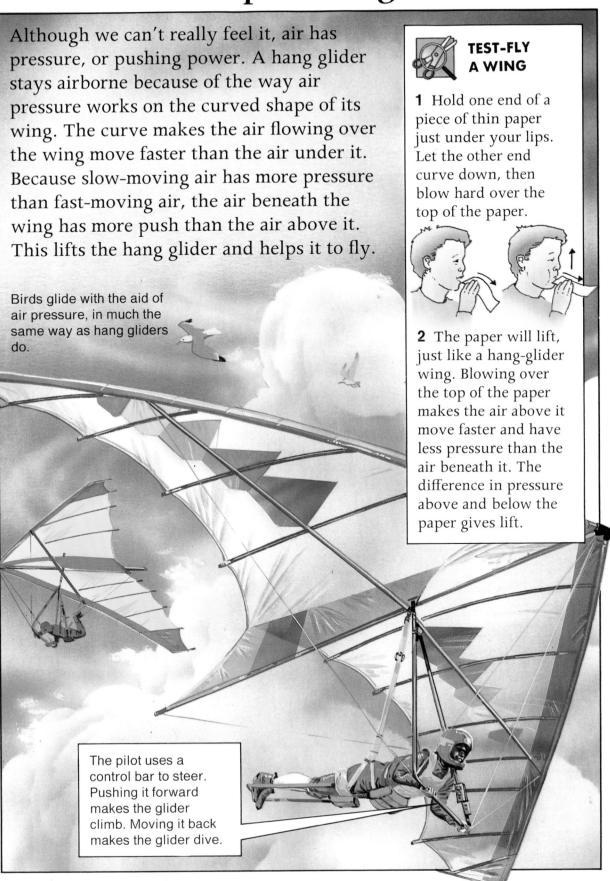

TEST-FLY A WING

1 Hold one end of a piece of thin paper just under your lips. Let the other end curve down, then blow hard over the top of the paper.

2 The paper will lift, just like a hang-glider wing. Blowing over the top of the paper makes the air above it move faster and have less pressure than the air beneath it. The difference in pressure above and below the paper gives lift.

The pilot uses a control bar to steer. Pushing it forward makes the glider climb. Moving it back makes the glider dive.

How fast does sound travel?

Sound is energy made when something vibrates, or moves backward and forward. The vibrations travel in waves, but they move at different speeds through different materials. At sea level, for example, sound waves travel through air at about 1,087 feet per second. They move at 4.5 times that speed through water.

Concorde is about 203 feet long from nose to tail. Its slender swept-back wings measure just over 83 feet across.

Concorde can cruise at around 1,450 miles per hour (mph), more than twice the speed of sound (sound travels faster in the thinner air high above Earth than it does at sea level).

The pilot can move the plane's nose into three different positions – for takeoff, for cruising, and for landing.

Powered by four jet engines, two under each wing, Concorde has cut usual flying times across the North Atlantic by half.

SOUND MESSAGES

Sound waves travel more easily through brick and stone than through the air. If you invent a code using sounds, you can send messages through walls. Stand with your ear to a wall of your house, and get a friend outside to tap out a message.

What is an echo?

Echoes are repeated sounds. They happen when sound waves are blocked by a hard surface, such as a mountainside or a cliff face. The waves bounce off and we hear the sound again. Echoes are loudest in enclosed areas such as tunnels because they bounce backward and forward from wall to wall.

Echoes happen when sound waves bounce back off a hard surface, such as a cliff face.

How do drums work?

A drum makes a sound when you hit it because it vibrates and sends out sound waves. Most drums are a tightly stretched sheet of skin or plastic over a hollow container. The hollow body of the drum makes noises louder because it traps the sound waves, making them bounce back-ward and forward inside it.

MAKING DRUMSTICKS

Drummers use different kinds of drumsticks to make a range of sounds. Try this for yourself – make drumsticks with all sorts of ends on them. Try wooden beads, cork, wool, a sponge, and a metal nut. What happens if you use a toothbrush?

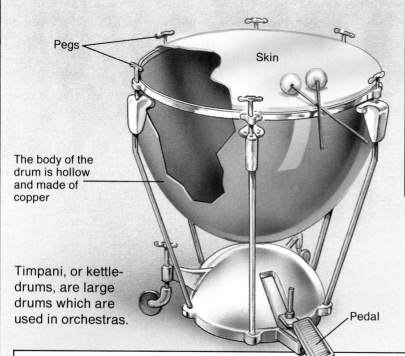

Pegs

Skin

The body of the drum is hollow and made of copper

Timpani, or kettle-drums, are large drums which are used in orchestras.

Pedal

Pressing the pedal or turning the pegs tightens the skin. The tighter the skin, the faster it vibrates when it's hit. When the skin vibrates faster, it produces higher notes.

DRUM FACTS

- A tabla is a set of two hand drums from northern India. Each drum has a different tone, or sound.

- Japanese drums are often rested on stands for playing. They are used during special religious services and theater performances.

- Indonesian drums have skins laced to the top and bottom ends. Making the lacing looser or tighter changes the tone of the drum.

How do recorders work?

All musical instruments have a part which vibrates and makes sound waves. When you blow into the mouthpiece of a recorder, you are pushing in a column of air which vibrates inside the recorder's body. Trumpets and flutes work in the same way.

BALLOON MUSIC

Blow up a balloon and hold the neck as shown below. Pull the balloon neck slowly out sideways to make sounds. To make different sounds, try pulling the balloon neck in and out.

How do guitars work?

The vibrating parts of a guitar are its strings. When you pluck the strings, the vibrations travel into the hollow body of the guitar. The body acts like the hollow part of a drum, to make the sound louder.

Guitar strings can be made tighter or looser by turning these pegs at the top of the neck.

Bridge

Strings

Peg

BODY

The tighter the guitar string, or the shorter, the higher the note it makes. Pressing a finger on a string shortens it and makes a higher note. Most guitars have 6 strings.

Sound hole

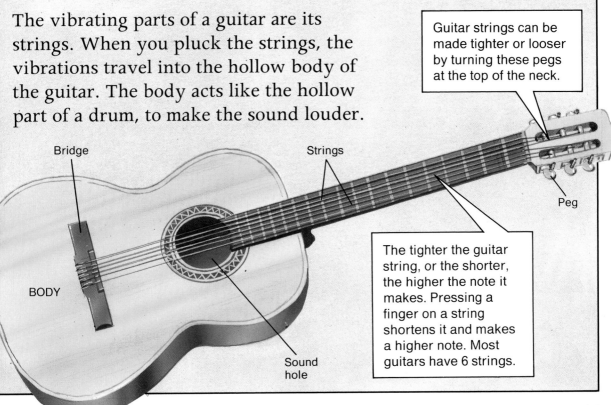

What is solar energy?

Solar energy is the heat and light given off by the sun. Much of the solar energy that reaches Earth bounces off again, back into space. Only about 15 percent of it is absorbed, or soaked up, by Earth's surface.

Solar energy can be collected by special panels and used to make electricity. Some countries have built giant solar collectors which produce enough electricity to power small towns.

SOLAR POWER FACTS

• The sun produces 100,000 times more energy than all the world's power stations put together.

• A solar-powered furnace in the French Pyrenees can produce temperatures of 7,200°F. It is used to melt metals.

• Spacecraft often make use of solar energy – the space shuttle Discovery has 84 solar panels.

The first World Solar Challenge, a race for solar cars, took place in 1987. The 23 entrants raced 1,865 miles, from Darwin in the north of Australia to Adelaide in the south. The winner, Sunraycer, averaged over 40 mph.

Some cars have been designed to run on solar energy. They have big solar panels to collect the sun's heat and light energy.

How many colors are there in rainbows?

Although most people can see seven colors in a rainbow – red, orange, yellow, green, blue, indigo, and violet – there are actually more than 100 different shades!

Rainbows form when sunlight passes through drops of water. Sunlight looks colorless and is called white light, but it is really made up of all the colors in a rainbow. The water drops separate white light into all its different colors. The seven main rainbow colors are called the spectrum.

RED
ORANGE
YELLOW
GREEN
BLUE
INDIGO
VIOLET

The water drops in the spray from a garden hose or sprinkler will often make a rainbow on a sunny day. You can also sometimes see the colors of the rainbow in soap bubbles and in thin patches of oil on a wet road.

SEEING WHITE LIGHT

1 With an adult's help, cut out a circle of white cardboard about 5 inches across. Make a hole in the middle big enough to take a short piece of pencil.

2 Divide the circle into seven equal sections and paint a different rainbow color in each one.

3 Put the pencil through the hole and fix it with modeling clay. Spin the pencil – the colors seem to combine so that you see white light.

Why do we see different colors?

We see things because light reflects, or bounces, off them into our eyes – that's why it's difficult to see anything in the dark. We see different colors because objects reflect some of the colors of white light and absorb, or soak up, others. Red things reflect red light and absorb most of the other colors in white light, for example.

 COLOR FACTS

- You can make all the colors of the rainbow by mixing red and green, green and blue, or blue and red light. Combining all three colors creates white light. Red, green, and blue are called the primary colors of light.

- Paint, ink, and crayons are like all other objects – they only reflect the light that falls on them. You can make all the rainbow colors by mixing red and yellow, yellow and blue, or blue and red paint. Red, yellow, and blue are the primary colors of paint.

Things look blue because they reflect blue light. They absorb the other colors of white light.

Things look black because they absorb all of the colors of white light.

How are shadows made?

Shadows happen when light can't shine through something. Light can't shine through your body, for example, so a shadow forms on the side of your body opposite to the light. Things that light can't shine through are called opaque. See-through things, like glass, are called transparent – light can shine through them and they don't cast strong shadows.

 SHADOW PICTURE GAME

Rooster

Rabbit

Donkey

With a flashlight and the help of a friend, you can make shadow pictures of your own. In a darkened room, hold your hands in the beam of light from the flashlight. Clasp your hands together and try moving your fingers and thumbs around to make different shapes.

Can light bend?

Light always travels in straight lines – it cannot bend, although sometimes it seems to. However, light travels at different speeds through different materials. It moves faster through air than it does through water, for example. When light changes speed, it alters direction slightly and appears to bend – you can see this if you look at drinking straws in water. This ''bending'' of light is called refraction.

 MAGIC MONEY

1 Put a cup on a flat surface and place a coin inside it. Looking at the coin, slowly move the cup away – just to the point where you can't see the coin.

2 Stay still, and ask a friend to pour some water slowly into the cup. You'll suddenly see the coin again as the water bends the light rays toward your eyes.

 Things appear to bend in water because light rays change direction slightly as their speed alters between the air and the water.

1

2

 DO YOU KNOW

Light also alters direction slightly and appears to bend when it passes through glass. You can see this if you hold a pencil behind a thick glass bowl so that half the pencil is above the bowl and half is below it. The pencil seems to bend at the edge of the bowl. This happens because the light rays are traveling more slowly through the glass bowl than through the air around it, and they change direction slightly as they pass into the glass.

What is a mirage?

On really hot days, you may see what look like shimmering pools of water on the road, even though the road is really completely dry! This trick of the light is a mirage. It happens because the air near the ground is hotter than the air above it, and because light travels at different speeds through air of different temperatures. As rays of sunlight pass into the hot air near the road, they are refracted, or "bent," and look like shimmering pools of water.

In the desert, a shimmering pool of water is often a mirage. It isn't water at all, but an image of the sky caused by light being refracted by warm air near the ground.

Desert travelers see mirages because light rays are refracted upward as they pass from cool air into warmer air near the ground. This makes distant things appear to be close.

DO YOU KNOW

Mirages happen near the North and South Poles because the air near the sea is colder than the air above it. Light rays change speed and refract downward as they travel from warmer into cooler air. This brings into view objects such as ships which are a long way off, making them look like they're floating in the sky!

How do glasses help people see?

When you see something, it's because light rays bounce off it and travel into your eyes. Each eye has a lens to focus, or sharpen, these light rays and make a clear picture. Because the lenses in some people's eyes don't focus sharply, they wear glasses with lenses in them to correct this.

 WATER-DROP LENS

1 With an adult's help, cut a circle about 1 inch in diameter into a piece of thin cardboard. Then stick a piece of cellophane tape

Cellophane

carefully across the hole.

2 Use a straw to put a drop of water on the tape, then look at something through the drop of water.

3 The water makes things look bigger, just like a lens does. If you look at the water drop from the side, you'll see that it is convex – it's fatter in the middle than at the edges.

CONCAVE LENS

Nearsighted people have difficulty seeing objects that are far away. Their glasses have lenses which are thinner in the middle than at the edges. Lenses this shape are called concave, and they make things look smaller.

Concave lens

CONVEX LENS

Farsighted people find it difficult to see things which are near to them. The lenses in their glasses are thicker in the middle than at the edges, and they make things look bigger. Lenses that are shaped like this are called convex.

Convex lens

How do telescopes work?

A simple telescope uses two lenses to make things look closer than they really are. A large lens collects and focuses light rays from something far away. Then a small lens makes the image larger again, until it can be seen clearly by the person using the telescope. Binoculars work like two small telescopes – one for each eye.

A large lens at the end of the telescope collects and focuses light from faraway objects.

The person using the telescope focuses on the image through a smaller lens called the eyepiece.

NEVER LOOK AT THE SUN

Never look directly at the sun, especially through a telescope, as its powerful rays will damage your eyes.

DO YOU KNOW

The first telescope was made by Hans Lipper-shey, a Dutchman who made eyeglasses. In 1608 he discovered that using two lenses to look at a church steeple made it seem much larger and closer.

In 1609, an Italian scientist named Galileo Galilei built the first telescope which was powerful enough to be used for studying the stars and the planets.

How do mirrors work?

Most mirrors are sheets of polished glass with a shiny coating of metal behind them. Light rays travel through the glass, but bounce off the mirror's metal coating because it isn't transparent. A reflection, or repeated image, then forms on the glass. This reflected image is what you see when you look in a mirror.

Not all mirrors are flat. Convex mirrors curve outward in the middle (like the back of a spoon) and make things look smaller. They reflect a much wider view than a normal mirror because of this. Car mirrors are convex and help drivers to see more of the road behind them.

Concave mirrors curve inward in the middle (like the front of a spoon) and make things look larger. Bathroom mirrors are often concave in shape.

 SPOON MIRRORS

1 Polish a large spoon with a soft cloth until it's shiny, then hold its back level with your eyes and about 8 inches away. You'll see a small fuzzy image of yourself.

2 Now do the same with the front of the spoon – the image will be upside down!

3 Spoons aren't real mirrors, so they don't make objects bigger and smaller in the same way as concave and convex mirrors do. Like these different mirrors, though, the two sides of a spoon (the back is convex and the front is concave) reflect light rays in opposite ways.

 DO YOU KNOW

Wave at yourself in a mirror using your left hand. Which hand is your reflection waving? Mirrors reverse, or swap, images so that the left side appears to be the right. Mirrors do this to images because of the way light rays bounce off them. The diagram below shows how it happens.

Light rays

Reflected light rays

Concave front

Convex back

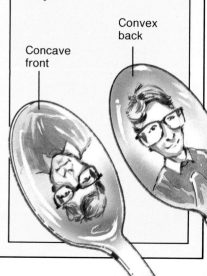

How do funhouse mirrors work?

Funhouse mirrors stretch and squeeze people into all sorts of funny shapes and sizes. This happens because they are made by mixing different types of mirror. Some parts are convex and make things look smaller; other parts are concave and make things look bigger. The convex parts squeeze, and the concave parts stretch!

Cats' eyes seem to shine in the dark because the lining of their eyes works like a mirror. It's called the tapetum and it reflects light.

 MIRROR CODE

Mirrors can help you send secret messages to your friends. Stand a mirror in front of a piece of paper and look in the mirror while you write. On the paper your writing will be upside down and back to front. Send your message to friends, and explain how they can read it using another mirror.

What are X-rays?

X-rays are invisible waves of energy, like sound or light waves. They are very powerful, and they can pass through flesh in much the same way that light travels through glass. Doctors use X-rays to take special photographs of people's insides.

Most X-rays pass through the body to hit a special photographic film, making it black.

X-rays cannot travel easily through bone, and a shadow of the bones forms on the X-ray photograph.

Gamma rays – highest frequency, shortest wavelength

X-rays

Ultraviolet rays

Visible light

Infrared rays

Microwaves

Radio waves – lowest frequency, longest wavelength

What are lasers?

Lasers strengthen light and make it shine in a narrow beam which is very powerful. A laser beam can cut a hole in a thick steel plate in seconds, for example. Low-powered lasers are used by doctors to carry out delicate operations. Lasers are also used in compact disk players and to create colorful lighting effects at concerts and stage shows.

LASER FACTS

● The first laser was built in 1960.

● Dentists sometimes use lasers instead of drills to remove decay from teeth.

In factories, lasers are used to cut metals and to weld, or join, them together.

● Some lasers are powerful enough to cut through diamonds – the hardest known stones in the world!

● Laser beams can be sent along hairlike glass fibers carrying radio, TV, or telephone messages.

What are holograms?

Holograms are a special type of photograph made with laser light. Normal photographs are two-dimensional – they have width and height. Holograms, on the other hand, have width, height, and depth and can be seen from all angles – they are three-dimensional. Holograms don't show the colors of the original object, though. They take their color from the laser beam instead.

Where does water go when it boils?

If you boil water in a saucepan or a kettle, it turns into an invisible gas called water vapor. Water boils when it reaches 212°F – it has to be this hot to become a gas. When the hot water vapor hits the cold air outside the kettle, however, it cools and turns back into tiny droplets of water. The steam that comes out of the kettle is like a mini-cloud made of these water droplets.

Steam forms when a kettle boils because the invisible gas water vapor is cooled by the cold air outside the kettle and turns back into a "cloud" of tiny water droplets.

 TURN AIR INTO WATER

Although we can't see it, air has the gas water vapor in it. You'll need a label-free can with a lid to prove this.

1 Polish the can with a cloth, then fill it with ice cubes. Put the lid on and dry the outside of the can.

2 Within minutes, a film of water droplets will appear on the can. This is because the ice makes the can so cold that some of the water vapor in the air around it cools and turns back into water droplets.

? DO YOU KNOW

Water can be a liquid, an invisible gas (water vapor), or a solid – ice is solid water.

What are geysers?

Geysers are scalding-hot fountains of steam and water. They happen from time to time when a deep crack in the ground fills with water, which is then heated by hot rocks deep below Earth's surface. The water at the bottom of the crack becomes super-hot and turns to gas and steam. This then explodes upward, pushing the water above it up and out of the crack as well.

DO YOU KNOW

The word "geyser" comes from the name of a famous geyser near Mount Hekla, an active volcano in southern Iceland. It's called the Stori Geysir, which is Icelandic for "great gusher."

GEYSER FACTS

● The USA's best-known geyser is Old Faithful in Yellowstone National Park. It raises a jet about 130 feet high.

● The tallest geyser ever known was New Zealand's Waimangu Geyser. In 1904, it squirted steam and water more than 1,470 feet into the sky – that's higher than the Empire State Building!

1 Geysers explode from time to time as fountains of scalding-hot steam and water.

2 They form when deep cracks open in Earth's surface and fill up with water.

3 Boiling-hot rocks deep below Earth's surface heat the water until it turns into gas and steam.

How do insects walk on water?

Not all insects can walk on water, of course, but the ones that do are supported by a force called surface tension. This is like a thin elastic skin which holds the surface of the water together. You can see this "skin" if you carefully fill a glass with water right to the brim. The water will curve above the rim of the glass, held by surface tension.

The water striders stretch out their legs to spread their weight over the surface "skin" of the water.

Water striders are insects which walk on water. The surface "skin" of the water dents a little around their feet, but it doesn't give way.

❓ DO YOU KNOW

Small drops of water are almost perfectly round because they are held together by surface tension. Bigger drops spread out because they are too heavy for surface tension to hold them together.

Why can we blow bubbles?

Adding soap to water weakens its surface tension and makes it even stretchier. If you dip a bubble-blowing wand into ordinary water, only a few water drops will stick to it. But if you dip the wand into soapy water, a glistening skin will form across the head of the wand. When you blow gently into this skin, it will stretch and stretch until it turns into an air-filled bubble and breaks free.

Blowing soapy bubbles will show you just how stretchy the "skin" on the surface of water can be.

 BLOWING BUBBLES

1 To make a bubble-blowing mixture, put 4 tablespoons of soap flakes into 4 cups of hot water (ask an adult to help you). Let the mixture stand for a day, then stir in a large teaspoonful of white sugar.

2 Bend a piece of thin wire into a wand. Dip this into the soap mixture and blow through it gently.

3 Try differently shaped wands. Cut slits about $\frac{1}{2}$ inch long into the end of a drinking straw, for example.

When does water freeze?

Water freezes when it gets too cold to stay liquid. Its freezing point is 32°F, and when it cools to this temperature, it turns into solid ice. The gas water vapor also freezes at 32°F – frost and snowflakes are frozen water vapor, in fact.

 CUTTING ICE

1 See how ice skates work for yourself. Tie a fork to each end of a piece of thin wire about 15 inches long.

2 Balance an ice cube on top of a bottle and hang the wire and forks over it.

3 Put the bottle in the fridge. The weight of the forks will make the wire pass through the ice cube without dividing it in two!

Ice skaters glide on a film of water which forms as their skates press down on the ice.

Why do ships float?

Anything will float if the amount of water it displaces, or pushes aside, weighs more than it does. Ships are helped to do this by their shape. You can prove this for yourself with a ball of modeling clay. If you put the clay into a bucket of water it will sink. Now take the clay out, dry it, and shape it into a hollow boat. Put it back into the water – this time it will float!

DO YOU KNOW

Ships can sink if they are overloaded, of course. The amount they can carry depends partly on the type of water they sail in and the weather. Every big ship has a mark on its side to show how low it can float in different types of water without sinking. This mark is called the Plimsoll line because it was invented by Samuel Plimsoll in 1876.

PLIMSOLL LINE

TF = tropical fresh water
F = fresh water
T = tropical seas
S = summer seas
W = winter seas
WNA = winter in North Atlantic

Ships can carry the heaviest loads in the warm fresh water of tropical regions. They can carry much less when sailing across the North Atlantic in cold winter weather.

This large tanker floats because even fully loaded it weighs less than the amount of water it displaces.

Can water flow uphill?

Although water can be forced upward – in a fountain or a geyser, for example – it usually flows downhill. All the water on Earth settles at the lowest level it can reach. Some of it collects in lakes, rivers, and seas. The rest soaks into the ground.

Water flows downhill because, like everything else on Earth, it is affected by gravity. This is the pulling force that tries to tug everything toward the center of Earth. Gravity keeps our feet on the ground and stops us from flying off into space.

DO YOU KNOW

When you weigh something, you are measuring the force with which gravity is pulling it down toward the center of Earth.

STRAW MAGIC

Here's a way to amaze your friends by stopping water from flowing downward.

1 Suck some water up into a straw and quickly put a finger over the top of it.

2 Hold your hand out, keeping the straw upright – the water will stay in the straw!

3 What happens when you take your finger off the top of the straw again?

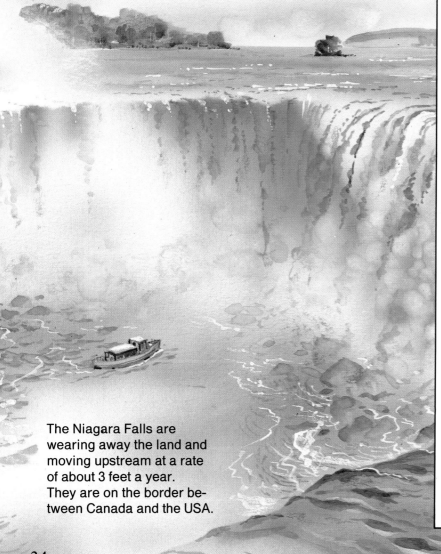

The Niagara Falls are wearing away the land and moving upstream at a rate of about 3 feet a year. They are on the border between Canada and the USA.

How do fountains and hoses work?

Fountains and hoses work because the water in them has pressure, or push, and putting water under pressure makes it flow more quickly. One way of putting water under pressure is to use a special sort of pump to compress, or squash, it. Fire engines have pumps which put water under very high pressure, making it shoot out in a fast-flowing jet.

FOUNTAIN FACTS

● The highest fountain in the world is at Fountain Hills, in Arizona. It can shoot 9 tons of water 560 feet into the air – that's higher than a 40-story office building!

Firefighting hoses are fixed to pumps on the fire engine. These put water from the hydrant under high pressure.

Hydrants are like taps which lead to water pipes under the street. A hose joins the hydrant to the fire engine's pumps.

Water flows faster and has more power when it's put under high pressure.

What is water power?

People have used the strength and power of moving water for hundreds of years. Water mills used the power of fast-flowing rivers to turn stones which ground wheat into flour. Today, hydroelectric power stations use the power of falling water to drive machines called generators to make electricity. Even the movement of tides and waves can now be used to drive generators and produce electricity.

 DAM FACTS

● The world's longest dam is the Yacyreta-Apipe Dam in South America. It is 45 miles long and 135 feet high.

● The highest dam is the Nurek Dam in the USSR (1,100 feet high and 1,975 feet long).

? DO YOU KNOW

Around 3 percent of the world's electricity is generated by falling water. Water is a renewable source of power – unlike oil, coal, and natural gas, it won't run out.

1 Giant sluice gates can be raised or lowered to control the amount of water flowing through them.

2 The dam wall has to be thick and strong so that it holds back all the water in the reservoir behind it.

Dam wall

3 Water from the reservoir thunders down huge tunnels toward the turbines in the power station.

DO YOU KNOW

Power stations can also be built in barriers across estuaries, where rivers meet the sea and are affected by its rising and falling tides.

As the tide rises (1) water flows in through the barrier, driving turbines to make electricity. Sluice gates trap the water behind the barrier at high tide.

When the tide drops (2), the sluice gates are opened, letting the water flow back through the turbines.

1

HIGH TIDE

Water flows in — Turbine

2

LOW TIDE

Water flows out

5 As they spin around, the turbines drive machines called generators which produce electricity.

Power station

4 The turbines are wheels with blades set into them. The force of the water rushing past spins them around.

What is acid rain?

Acid rain is a poison which is polluting, or dirtying, the land and the water on Earth. When coal, oil, and natural gas are burned, gases containing sulfur and nitrogen are given off. These gases combine with the moisture in the air to make acid rain or snow. When this falls on the land, it enters the soil and harms the growth of plants. Acid rain is also poisoning lakes, killing the plants and animals that live in them.

ACID RAIN FACTS

● Acid rain can be 1,000 times as acidic, or sour, as normal rain. It is carried across countries and between continents by wind.

● The effect of acid rain on lakes and rivers was first noticed in Sweden, where around 10% of lakes no longer have live fish in them.

Coal, oil, and natural gas are burned as fuel in factories and power stations, as well as in homes. This produces the gases that make acid rain.

Useful words

Atmosphere   The air that surrounds Earth in a layer about 600 miles deep. It is largely made up of the gases nitrogen and oxygen, but it also has small amounts of water vapor and other gases in it, as well as salt, dust, and dirt.

Carbon dioxide   One of the gases in the atmosphere. About 0.03% of the air is carbon dioxide gas. Plants use carbon dioxide to help make their food.

Compress   To squeeze or squash something into a small space.

Concave   Curved inward. A concave lens is thinner in the middle than at the edges.

Convex   Curved outward. A convex lens is fatter in the middle than at the edges.

Energy   Power which is being sent out; the sun gives out heat and light energy, for example.

Lens   Lenses are used to make things look bigger or smaller. They are usually made of a transparent substance such as glass or plastic. Each of your eyes has a lens in it which is made of a material called protein.

Opaque   Something which won't let light through, and which we can't see through.

Oxygen   About 21% of the air is made up of this gas. Humans and all other animals on Earth need to take or breathe oxygen into their bodies in order to live. Oxygen passes into our blood and, with the food we eat, gives us energy to live and grow.

Pollution   The dirtying of air, water, or the soil.

Pressure   Another word for push. Both air and water have pressure, although we can't usually feel it.

Reflect   To bounce off or throw back – when sound waves bounce off a hard cliff face, for example, or rays of light bounce off something opaque.

Refraction   The change in speed and direction of light rays at the point where two different substances (such as air and water) meet, and where light appears to bend. Refraction happens because light travels at different speeds through different materials.

Surface tension   The thin, stretchy ''skin'' on water and other liquids.

Transparent   Something which is see-through.

Vibrate   To shake, or move backward and forward.

Water vapor   The invisible gas which water turns into when it is heated to a temperature of 212°F.

Index